ITALIAN HIGH RENAISSANCE AND
BAROQUE SCULPTURE

AN INTRODUCTION
TO ITALIAN SCULPTURE

BY

JOHN POPE-HENNESSY

PART I

ITALIAN GOTHIC SCULPTURE

PART II

ITALIAN RENAISSANCE SCULPTURE

PART III

ITALIAN HIGH RENAISSANCE AND BAROQUE SCULPTURE

IN THREE VOLUMES

JOHN POPE-HENNESSY

ITALIAN HIGH RENAISSANCE AND BAROQUE SCULPTURE

PLATES

PHAIDON PRESS

1963

MADE IN GREAT BRITAIN

PRINTED BY HUNT · BARNARD AND COMPANY LIMITED

AT THE SIGN OF THE DOLPHIN · AYLESBURY · BUCKS

CONTENTS

THE PLATES

1. Michelangelo: ANGEL. S. Domenico Maggiore, Bologna. Marble (H. 51.5 cm.).

2. Michelangelo: THE BATTLE OF THE CENTAURS. Casa Buonarroti, Florence. Marble (84.5×90.5 cm. overall).

3. Michelangelo: CHILD CHRIST (detail of Figure 5). Royal Academy of Arts, London. Marble (Diameter overall 109 cm.).

4. Michelangelo: THE PITTI MADONNA. Museo Nazionale, Florence. Marble (85.5 × 82 cm).

5. Michelangelo: VIRGIN (detail of Figure 5). Royal Academy of Arts, London. Marble (Diameter overall 109 cm.).

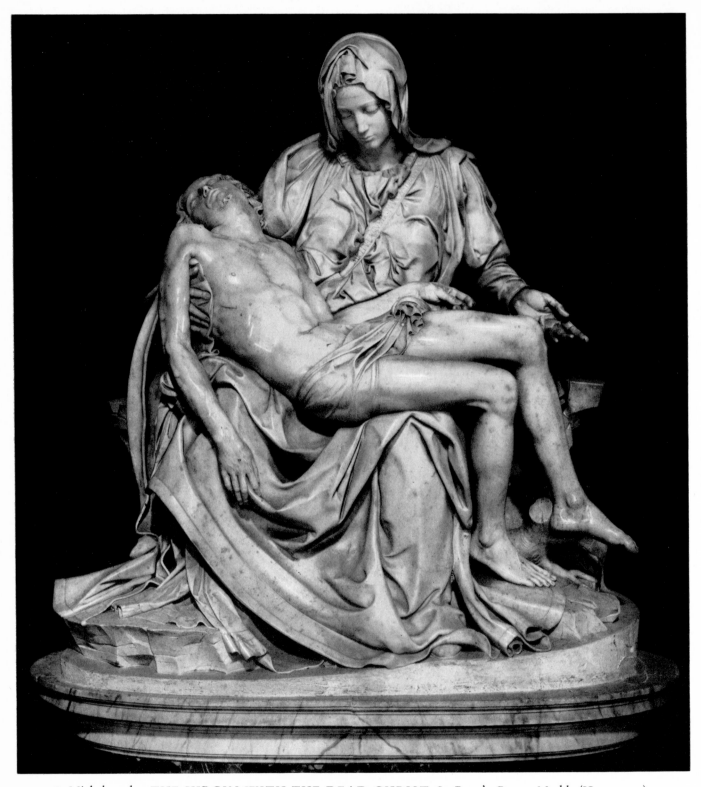

6. Michelangelo: THE VIRGIN WITH THE DEAD CHRIST. St. Peter's, Rome, Marble (H. 174 cm.).

7. Michelangelo: VIRGIN AND CHILD. Notre Dame, Bruges. Marble
(H. with base 128 cm.).

8. Michelangelo: CHILD CHRIST (detail of Plate 7). Notre Dame, Bruges. Marble.

9. Michelangelo: ST. PETER (detail of Figure 4). Duomo, Siena. Marble (H. overall ca. 120 cm.).

10. Michelangelo: BACCHUS. Museo Nazionale, Florence. Marble (H. 203 cm.).

11. Michelangelo: SATYR (detail of Plate 10). Museo Nazionale, Florence. Marble.

12. Michelangelo: D A V I D. Accademia, Florence. Marble (H. 434 cm.).

13. Michelangelo: HEAD OF DAVID (detail of Plate 12). Accademia, Florence.

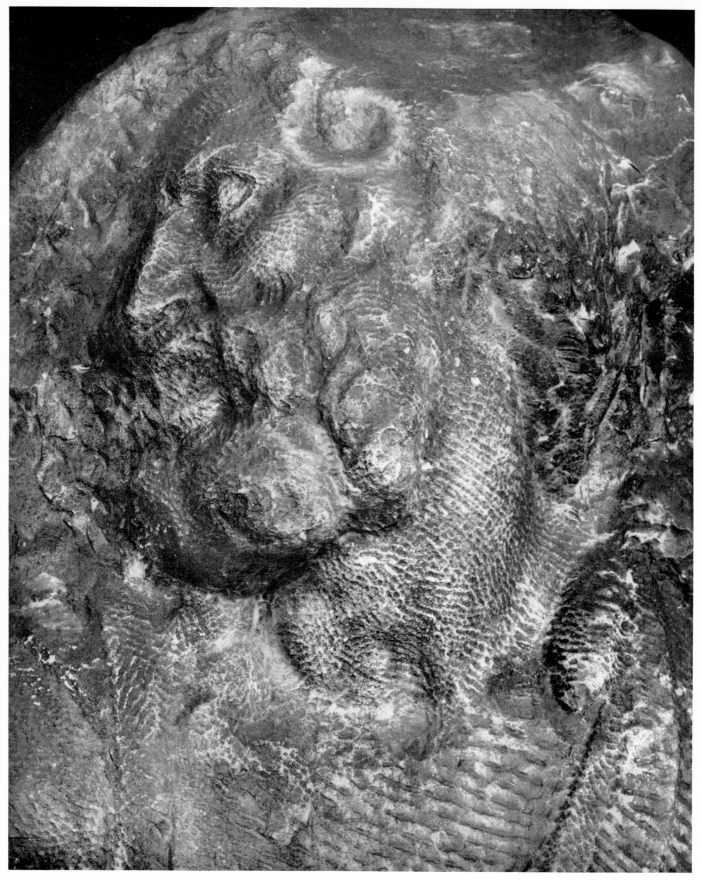

14. Michelangelo: HEAD OF ST. MATTHEW (detail of Figure 9). Accademia, Florence. Marble (H. overall 271 cm.).

15. Michelangelo: MOSES (detail of Figure 30). S. Pietro in Vincoli, Rome. Marble (H. overall 235 cm.).

16A. Michelangelo: THE REBELLIOUS SLAVE. Louvre, Paris. Marble (H. 215 cm.).

16B. Michelangelo: THE DYING SLAVE. Louvre, Paris. Marble (H. 229 cm.).

17A. Michelangelo: THE YOUNG SLAVE. Accademia, Florence. Marble (H. 256 cm.).
17B. Michelangelo: THE ATLAS SLAVE. Accademia, Florence. Marble (H. 277 cm.).

18. Michelangelo: THE BEARDED SLAVE. Accademia, Florence.
Marble (H. 263 cm.).

19. Michelangelo: THE AWAKENING SLAVE. Accademia, Florence.
Marble (H. 267 cm.).

20. Michelangelo: VIRGIN AND CHILD. Medici Chapel, Florence. Marble (H. 226 cm.).

21. Michelangelo: THE GENIUS OF VICTORY. Palazzo Vecchio, Florence. Marble (H. 261 cm.).

22. Michelangelo: APOLLO. Museo Nazionale, Florence.
Marble (H. 146 cm.).

25. Michelangelo: LORENZO DE' MEDICI (detail of Figure 18). Medici Chapel, Florence.
Marble (H. 178 cm.).

26. Michelangelo: END OF SARCOPHAGUS (detail of Figure 17). Medici Chapel, Florence. Marble.

27. Michelangelo: BOX HELD BY LORENZO DE' MEDICI (detail of Plate 25). Medici Chapel, Florence. Marble.

28. Michelangelo: NIGHT (detail of Figure 17). Medici Chapel, Florence. Marble (L. 194 cm.).

29. Michelangelo: DAY (detail of Figure 17). Medici Chapel, Florence. Marble (L. 185 cm.).

30. Michelangelo: MASK (detail of Plate 28). Medici Chapel, Florence. Marble.

31. Michelangelo: DAY (detail of Figure 17). Medici Chapel, Florence. Marble.

32. Michelangelo: EVENING (detail of Figure 18). Medici Chapel, Florence. Marble (L. 195 cm.).

33. Michelangelo: MORNING (detail of Figure 18). Medici Chapel, Florence. Marble (L. 203 cm.).

34. Michelangelo: LEAH (detail of Figure 30). S. Pietro in Vincoli, Rome. Marble (H. 209 cm.).

35. Michelangelo: RACHEL (detail of Figure 30). S. Pietro in Vincoli, Rome. Marble (H. 197 cm.).

36. Michelangelo: HEADS OF CHRIST AND NICODEMUS (detail of Figure 35). Duomo, Florence. Marble (H. overall 226 cm.).

37. Michelangelo: HEAD OF NICODEMUS (detail of Figure 35). Duomo, Florence. Marble.

38. Rustici: A LEVITE (detail of Figure 39). Baptistry, Florence. Bronze (H. overall 265 cm. with base).

39. Rustici: HEAD OF ST. JOHN THE BAPTIST (detail of Figure 39). Baptistry, Florence. Bronze
(H. overall 265 cm. with base).

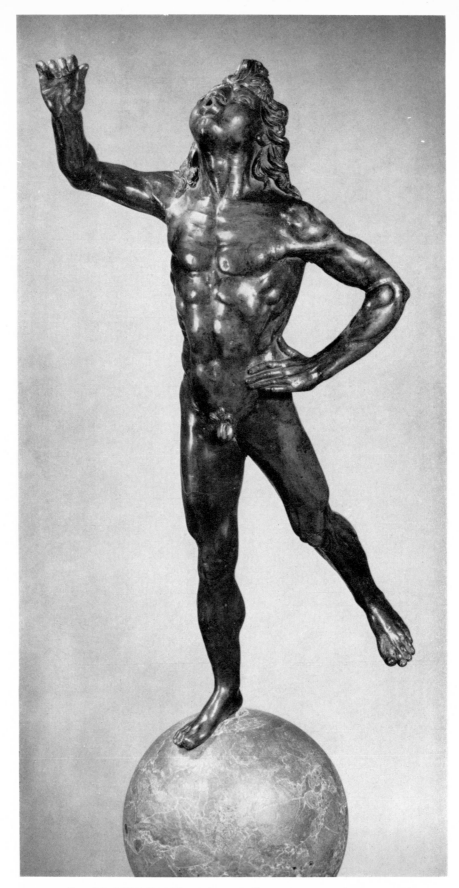

40. Rustici: MERCURY. Private Collection. Bronze (H. 49.5 cm.).

41. Lorenzetti: CHRIST AND THE WOMAN TAKEN IN ADULTERY (detail of Figure 79).
S. Maria del Popolo, Rome. Bronze (65.5×212 cm. overall).

42. Andrea Sansovino: VIRGIN AND CHILD. Duomo, Genoa. Marble.

43. Andrea Sansovino: THE BAPTISM OF CHRIST. Baptistry, Florence. Marble (H. of Christ 282 cm. with base; H. of Baptist 260 cm. with base).

44. Andrea Sansovino: TEMPERANCE (detail of Figure 58). S. Maria del Popolo, Rome. Marble (H. 121 cm.).

45. Andrea Sansovino: HOPE (detail of Figure 57). S. Maria del Popolo, Rome. Marble (H. 107 cm.).

46. Andrea Sansovino: THE HOLY FAMILY (detail of Figure 81). Basilica della Santa Casa, Loreto. Marble.

47. Andrea Sansovino: VIRGIN ANNUNCIATE (detail of Figure 80). Basilica della Santa Casa, Loreto. Marble.

IESV·DEO·DEIQ·FILIO·MATRI
VIRGINI·ANNÆ·AVIÆ·MATERNÆ·
IO·CORICIVS·EX·GERMANIS
LVCVMBVRG·PROT·APOST·DDD·
PERPETVO·SACRIFICIO·DOTEM
VASA·VESTES·TRIBVIT·MDXII

48. Andrea Sansovino: VIRGIN AND CHILD WITH ST. ANNE. S. Agostino, Rome.
Marble (H. of statue 125 cm.; H. with plinth 195 cm.).

49. Jacopo Sansovino: VIRGIN AND CHILD. S. Agostino, Rome. Marble.

50. Jacopo Sansovino: BACCHUS. Museo Nazionale, Florence. Marble (H. 146 cm.).

51. Jacopo Sansovino: ST. JAMES. Duomo, Florence. Marble.

52. Giovanni da Nola: MARIA OSORIO PIMENTEL (detail of Figure 64). S. Giacomo degli Spagnuoli, Naples. Marble.

53. Girolamo Santacroce: VIRGIN AND CHILD. S. Maria a Cappella Vecchia, Naples.
Marble.

54. Giovanni da Nola: THE LAMENTATION OVER THE DEAD CHRIST. S. Maria delle Grazie a Caponapoli, Naples. Marble (figurated area 100 × 165 cm.).

55. Francesco da Sangallo: MONUMENT OF ANGELO MARZI. SS. Annunziata, Florence. Marble (L. of effigy 194 cm.).

56. Francesco da Sangallo: VIRGIN AND CHILD WITH ST. ANNE. Or San Michele, Florence. Marble.

57. Montorsoli: SCYLLA (detail of Figure 96). Museo Nazionale, Messina. Marble (H. 180 cm.).

58. Tribolo: PAN. Museo Nazionale, Florence. Bronze (H. 26 cm.).

59. Tribolo: PUTTI WITH GEESE detail of Figure 92). Villa Reale di Castello. Marble.

60. Tribolo: THE ASSUMPTION OF THE VIRGIN (detail of Figure 83). S. Petronio, Bologna. Marble (W. irregular, ca. 250 cm.).

61. Pierino da Vinci: COSIMO I AS PATRON OF PISA. Museo Vaticano, Rome. Marble (73.5 × 160 cm.).

62. Pierino da Vinci: SAMSON AND A PHILISTINE. Palazzo Vecchio, Florence.
Marble (H. ca. 223 cm.).

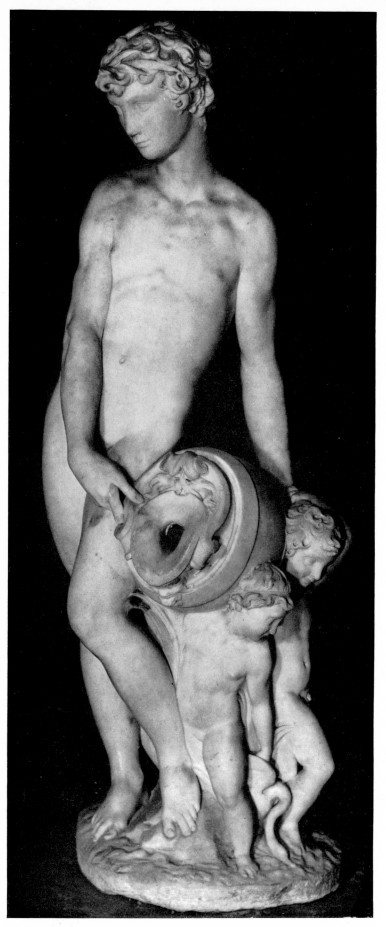

63. Pierino da Vinci: RIVER GOD. Louvre, Paris. Marble (H. 135 cm.).

64. Bandinelli: HERCULES AND CACUS. Piazza della Signoria, Florence. Marble.

65. Bandinelli: THE DEAD CHRIST WITH NICODEMUS. SS. Annunziata, Florence. Marble.

66. Bandinelli: TWO PROPHETS (detail of Figure 87). Duomo, Florence. Marble (H. inside moulding 96.5 cm.).

67. Giovanni Bandini: ARCHITECTURE (detail of Figure 67). S. Croce, Florence. Marble.

68. Bandinelli: COSIMO I DE' MEDICI. Museo Nazionale, Florence. Marble (H. 91 cm.).

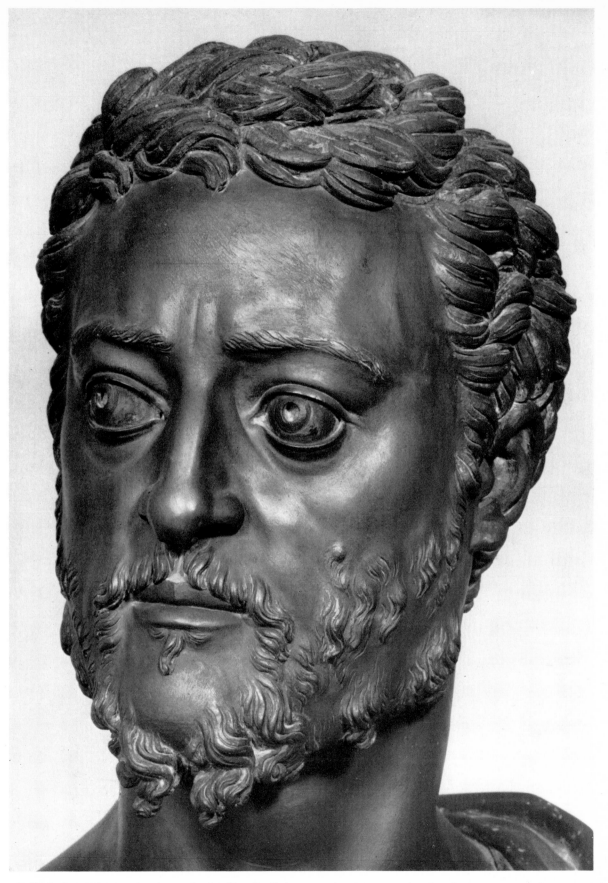

69. Cellini: COSIMO I DE' MEDICI (detail of Figure 121). Museo Nazionale, Florence. Bronze (H. 110 cm.).

70. Cellini: PERSEUS. Loggia dei Lanzi, Florence. Bronze (H. 320 cm.).

71. Cellini: HEAD OF MEDUSA (detail of Plate 70).
Loggia dei Lanzi, Florence. Bronze.

72. Cellini: CRUCIFIED CHRIST (detail of Figure 66). Church of the Escorial. Marble (H. overall 185 cm.).

73. Ammanati: VICTORY. Museo Nazionale, Florence. Marble (H. 262 cm.).

74. Ammanati: MARINE GOD (detail of Figure 98). Piazza della Signoria, Florence. Bronze.

75. Ammanati: MONUMENT OF ANTONIO DEL MONTE (detail of Figure 69). S. Pietro in Montorio, Rome. Marble.

76. Vincenzo Danti: SALOME (detail of Figure 40). Baptistry, Florence. Bronze (H. 243 cm. with base).

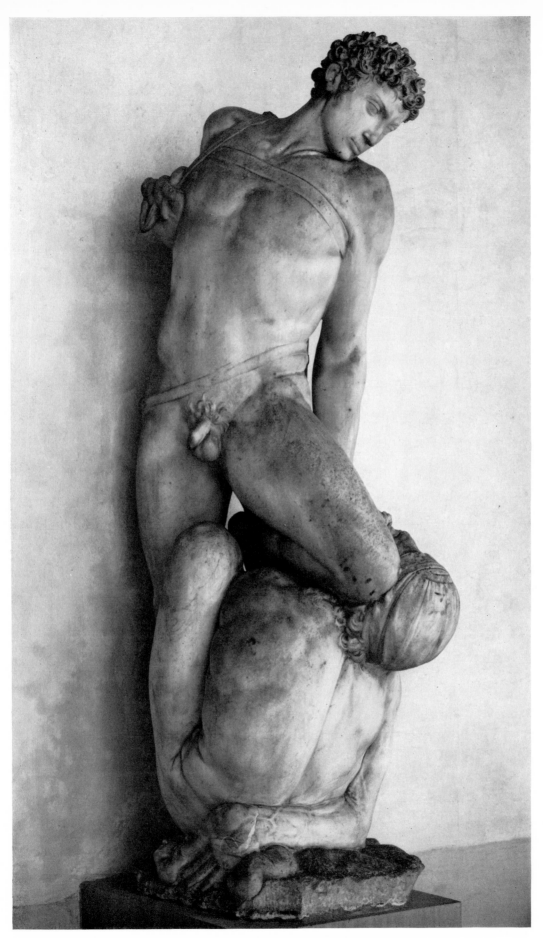

77. Vincenzo Danti: HONOUR TRIUMPHANT OVER FALSEHOOD.
Museo Nazionale, Florence. Marble.

78. Vincenzo Danti: VENUS ANADYOMENE. Palazzo Vecchio, Florence. Bronze (H. 98 cm.).

79. Giovanni Bologna: APOLLO. Palazzo Vecchio, Florence. Bronze (H. 88 cm.).

80. Giovanni Bologna: HEAD OF BACCHUS (detail of Figure 52). Borgo San Jacopo, Florence. Bronze (H. overall 228 cm.).

81. Giovanni Bologna: HEAD OF NEPTUNE (detail of Figure 94). Piazza Nettuno, Bologna.
Bronze (H. of central figure ca. 335 cm.).

82. Giovanni Bologna: SAMSON AND A PHILISTINE. Victoria & Albert Museum, London.
Marble (H. 210 cm.).

83. Giovanni Bologna: THE RIVER EUPHRATES (detail of Figure 95). Boboli Gardens, Florence. Marble.

84. Giovanni Bologna: CHRIST (detail of Figure 73) Duomo, Lucca. Marble (H. ca. 230 cm.).

85. Giovanni Bologna: THE RAPE OF THE SABINES. Loggia dei Lanzi, Florence. Marble (H. ca. 410 cm.).

86. Giovanni Bologna: THE RAPE OF THE SABINES. Loggia dei Lanzi, Florence. Bronze (75×90 cm.).

87. Giovanni Bologna: ECCE HOMO. University, Genoa. Bronze (47×71 cm.).

88. Giovanni Bologna: CHARITY. University, Genoa. Bronze (H. 175 cm.).

89. Giovanni Bologna: ANGEL (detail of Figure 75). S. Marco, Florence. Bronze.

90. Giovanni Bologna: MONUMENT OF COSIMO I DE' MEDICI. Piazza della Signoria, Florence.
Bronze (H. ca. 450 cm.).

91. Giovanni Bologna: HERCULES AND THE CENTAUR. Loggia dei Lanzi, Florence.
Marble (H. ca. 270 cm.).

92. Giovanni Bologna: ST. ANTONINUS. S. Marco, Florence. Bronze (L. 179.5 cm.).

93. Giovanni Caccini: THE ANNUNCIATION (detail of Figure 90). Duomo, Pisa. Bronze.

94. Francavilla: MOSES (detail of Figure 76). S. Croce, Florence. Marble.

95. Francavilla: PRISONER. Louvre, Paris. Bronze (H. 155 cm.).

96. Pietro Tacca: SLAVE (detail of Figure 60). Piazza della Darsena, Leghorn. Bronze.

97. Pietro Tacca: FERDINAND I DE' MEDICI (detail of Figure 77). Cappella dei Principi, Florence. Gilt bronze.

98. Giacomo and Guglielmo della Porta: ALTAR OF THE APOSTLES (detail of Figure 143).
Duomo, Genoa. Marble.

99. Guglielmo della Porta: JUSTICE (detail of Figure 145). St. Peter's, Rome. Marble.

100. Guglielmo della Porta: POPE PAUL III (detail of Figure 145). St. Peter's, Rome. Bronze.

101. Guglielmo della Porta: POPE PAUL III. Museo Nazionale di Capodimonte, Naples. Marble (H. 75 cm.).

102. Annibale Fontana: VIRGIN OF THE ASSUMPTION. S. Maria presso S. Celso, Milan. Marble.

103. Leone Leoni: GIAN GIACOMO DE' MEDICI (detail of Figure 70). Duomo, Milan. Bronze.

104. Leone Leoni: SATYR ATTACKED BY LIONS. Casa degli Omenoni, Milan. Stone.

105. Leone Leoni: BARBARIAN CAPTIVES. Casa degli Omenoni, Milan. Stone.

106. Leone Leoni: MARY OF HUNGARY. Prado, Madrid. Bronze (H. 166 cm.).

107. Pompeo Leoni: TOMB OF THE EMPEROR CHARLES V. Church of the Escorial. Bronze.

108. Jacopo Sansovino: PEACE (detail of Figure 101). Piazza San Marco, Venice. Bronze (H. 149 cm.).

109. Jacopo Sansovino: APOLLO (detail of Figure 101). Piazza San Marco, Venice. Bronze (H. 149 cm.).

110. Jacopo Sansovino: THE RESURRECTION (detail of Figure 113). St. Mark's, Venice. Bronze
(relief inside moulding 62 × 59 cm.).

III. Jacopo Sansovino: ST. MARK HEALING A WOMAN POSSESSED OF A DEVIL. St. Mark's, Venice.
Bronze (50×66 cm.).

112. Jacopo Sansovino: THE MIRACLE OF THE MAIDEN CARILLA (detail of Figure 114). S. Antonio, Padua.
Marble.

113. Jacopo Sansovino: NEPTUNE. Palazzo Ducale, Venice. Marble.

114. Jacopo Sansovino: ST. JOHN THE BAPTIST.
S. Maria dei Frari, Venice. Marble (H. ca. 120 cm.).

115. Jacopo Sansovino: ALLEGORY OF THE REDEMPTION. St. Mark's, Venice. Gilt bronze (43×37 cm.).

116. Jacopo Sansovino: HEAD OF TOMMASO RANGONE (detail of Figure 116). S. Giuliano, Venice. Bronze.

117. Danese Cattaneo: ALLEGORICAL SCENE (detail of Figure 112). SS. Giovanni e Paolo, Venice. Bronze (76×76 cm.).

118. Jacopo Sansovino: JUPITER. Kunsthistorisches Museum, Vienna. Bronze (H. 43 cm.).

119. Danese Cattaneo: FORTUNA. Museo Nazionale, Florence. Bronze (H. 50 cm.).

120. Danese Cattaneo and Girolamo Campagna: DOGE LEONARDO LOREDANO AND THE MILITARY
MIGHT OF THE VENETIAN REPUBLIC (detail of Figure 112). SS. Giovanni e Paolo, Venice. Marble.

121. Danese Cattaneo: THE RISEN CHRIST (detail of Figure 106). S. Anastasia, Verona. Marble (H. 190 cm.).

122. Girolamo Campagna: ANGEL OF THE ANNUNCIATION (detail of Figure 118). Castelvecchio, Verona.
Bronze (H. 213 cm.).

123. Girolamo Campagna: GOD THE FATHER IN BENEDICTION WITH THE FOUR EVANGELISTS.
S. Giorgio Maggiore, Venice. Bronze.

124. Vittoria: TOMMASO RANGONE. Ateneo Veneto, Venice. Bronze (H. 81 cm.).

125. Vittoria: ST. ROCH (detail of Figure 110). S. Salvatore, Venice. Marble (H. 175 cm.).

126. Vittoria: ST. SEBASTIAN (detail of Figure 109). S. Francesco della Vigna, Venice.
Marble (H. 171 cm.).

127. Vittoria: ST. SEBASTIAN (detail of Figure 110). S. Salvatore, Venice. Marble (M. 170 cm.).

128. Vittoria: ST. JEROME. S. Maria dei Frari, Venice. Marble (H. 192 cm.).

The inscription on the base reads: ALEXANDER · VICTORIA · F

129. Vittoria: ST. JEROME. SS. Giovanni e Paolo, Venice. Marble (H. 169 cm.).

130. Vittoria: ST. JOHN THE BAPTIST. S. Francesco della Vigna, Venice.
Bronze (H. 71 cm.).

131. Vittoria: NEPTUNE WITH A SEA-HORSE.
Victoria & Albert Museum, London. Bronze (H. 49.5 cm.).

132. Tiziano Aspetti: FAITH. S. Antonio, Padua. Bronze (H. 100 cm.).

133. Niccolò Roccatagliata: ST. STEPHEN. S. Giorgio Maggiore, Venice. Bronze (H. 60.1 cm.).

134. Bastiano Torrigiani: POPE SIXTUS V. Ehem. Staatliche Museen, Berlin. Bronze. (H. 70 cm.).

135. Valsoldo: POPE SIXTUS V (detail of Figure 149). S. Maria Maggiore, Rome. Marble.

136. Niccolò Cordieri: DAVID. S. Maria Maggiore, Rome. Marble.

137. Pietro Bernini: ST. JOHN THE BAPTIST. S. Andrea della Valle, Rome. Marble.

138. Pietro Bernini: THE ASSUMPTION OF THE VIRGIN. S. Maria Maggiore, Rome. Marble.

139. Gian Lorenzo Bernini:
AENEAS, ANCHISES AND ASCANIUS LEAVING TROY.
Galleria Borghese, Rome. Marble (H. 220 cm.).

140. Gian Lorenzo Bernini: THE RAPE OF PROSERPINE.
Galleria Borghese, Rome. Marble (H. 225 cm.).

141. Gian Lorenzo Bernini: HEAD OF DAVID (detail of Figure 157). Galleria Borghese, Rome.
Marble (H. overall 170 cm.).

142. Gian Lorenzo Bernini: APOLLO AND DAPHNE. Galleria Borghese, Rome. Marble (H. without base 243 cm.).

143. Gian Lorenzo Bernini: S. BIBIANA (detail of Figure 162). S. Bibiana, Rome. Marble.

144. Gian Lorenzo Bernini: MONSIGNOR FRANCESCO BARBERINI. National Gallery of Art, Washington
(Samuel H. Kress Collection). Marble (H. 79.2 cm.).

145. Gian Lorenzo Bernini: POPE URBAN VIII. Heirs of Prince Enrico Barberini, Rome. Marble (H. 83 cm.).

146. Gian Lorenzo Bernini: MONUMENT OF POPE URBAN VIII. St. Peter's, Rome. Marble and bronze.

147. Gian Lorenzo Bernini: MONUMENT OF POPE ALEXANDER VII. St. Peter's, Rome. Marble and bronze.

148. Gian Lorenzo Bernini: CARDINAL SCIPIONE BORGHESE. Galleria Borghese, Rome. Marble (H. 78 cm.).

149. Gian Lorenzo Bernini: FRANCESCO I D'ESTE. Pinacoteca Estense, Modena. Marble (H. with base 100 cm.).

150. Gian Lorenzo Bernini: ANGEL WITH A LANCE (detail of Figure 163). S. Maria della Vittoria, Rome. Marble.

151. Gian Lorenzo Bernini: HEAD OF ST. TERESA (detail of Figure 163). S. Maria della Vittoria, Rome. Marble.

152. Gian Lorenzo Bernini: TRUTH UNVEILED. Galleria Borghese, Rome. Marble (H. 280 cm.).

153. Gian Lorenzo Bernini and Giacomo Antonio Fancelli: THE RIVER NILE (detail of Figure 174).
Piazza Navona, Rome. Marble.

154. Gian Lorenzo Bernini: ST. AUGUSTINE (detail of Figure 166). St. Peter's, Rome. Bronze.

155. Gian Lorenzo Bernini: THE CHAIR OF ST. PETER (detail of Figure 166). St. Peter's, Rome. Bronze.

156. Gian Lorenzo Bernini: ST. JEROME. Duomo, Siena. Marble (H. 195 cm.).

157. Gian Lorenzo Bernini: ANGEL WITH THE SUPERSCRIPTION. S. Andrea della Fratte, Rome. Marble.

158. Gian Lorenzo Bernini: THE DEATH OF THE BEATA LODOVICA ALBERTONI. S. Francesco a Ripa, Rome. Marble.

159. Maderno: ST. CECILIA. S. Cecilia in Trastevere, Rome. Marble.

160. Duquesnoy: ST. ANDREW. St. Peter's, Rome. Marble.

161. Francesco Mochi: ST. VERONICA. St. Peter's, Rome. Marble.

162. Francesco Mochi: EQUESTRIAN MONUMENT OF ALESSANDRO FARNESE (detail of Figure 140). Piazza Cavalli, Piacenza. Bronze.

163. Francesco Mochi: EQUESTRIAN MONUMENT OF ALESSANDRO FARNESE (detail of Figure 140). Piazza Cavalli, Piacenza. Bronze.

164. Algardi: CARDINAL LAUDIVIO ZACCHIA. Kaiser Friedrich Museum, Berlin. Marble
(H. without base 70 cm.).

165. Algardi: POPE INNOCENT X. Palazzo dei Conservatori, Rome. Bronze.

166. Algardi: MONUMENT OF POPE LEO XI. St. Peter's, Rome. Marble.

167. Algardi: THE MEETING OF ATTILA AND POPE LEO THE GREAT (detail of Figure 165).
St. Peter's, Rome. Marble.

168. Algardi: THE MARTYRDOM OF ST. PAUL. S. Paolo, Bologna. Marble (H. with base 286 cm.).